12/95

Trees

A HARPERCOLLINS NATURE STUDY BOOK

Trees

by Jonathan Pine

illustrated by Ken Joudrey

HarperCollins*Publishers*

To Marcel and Mimi and Claire Liberty,
living in Trenton, loving all trees
—J. P.

In loving memory of my mother
and for my father's support
and to Danika, our bright future.
—K. J.

Also in the
HarperCollins Nature Study Series:
Backyard Birds / Tide Pools / Wetlands

The illustrations in this book were painted with oils
on illustration board.

Trees
Text copyright © 1995 by Jan-Paul Malocsay
Illustrations copyright © 1995 by Ken Joudrey
All rights reserved. No part of this book may be used or reproduced in
any manner whatsoever without written permission except in the case of
brief quotations embodied in critical articles and reviews.
Printed in Mexico.
For information address HarperCollins
Children's Books, a division of HarperCollins Publishers,
10 East 53rd Street, New York, NY 10022.

Library of Congress Cataloging-in-Publication Data
Pine, Jonathan.
   Trees / by Jonathan Pine ; illustrated by Ken Joudrey.
      p.   cm. — (A HarperCollins nature study book)
   Includes bibliographical references.
   Summary: Introduces seven trees commonly found in North America,
and the importance of trees in our global environment.
   ISBN 0-06-021468-6. — ISBN 0-06-021469-4 (lib. bdg.)
   1. Trees—Juvenile literature.   2. Trees—North America—Juvenile
literature.   [1. Trees.]   I. Joudrey, Ken, ill.   II. Title.   III. Series.
QK475.8.P56   1995   93-3136
582.16—dc20   CIP
                                                                      AC

1 2 3 4 5 6 7 8 9 10
❖
First Edition

Contents

Greening and Growing for the Longest Time

TREES are the friendly giants of earth. They make dinosaurs and whales look small. Trees also outlive all other living things. Some kinds live for hundreds of years. A few survive for thousands!

A tree is a plant that builds up strength by growing wood. Each year it adds new layers just under the bark. This busily growing wood carries water and food all up and

down the tree. It strengthens roots to support the tree and search for water and nutrients. It forms more twigs to hold out more leaves.

The leaves of all green plants use the sun to make their food. Trees grow large to catch the light with as many leaves as possible. The biggest, oldest trees in the world began with the tiny green leaf a seed sends up.

That leaf and all that followed needed light and water, soil and climate, right for its kind of tree.

Any big old tree is a joy to see. It reaches up so high and out so far with all its limbs and leaves. So many wild things live up there. And so do we somehow. Our windows look at trees. Trees seem to share our thoughts and dreams. Their branches seem to catch the moon.

No wonder we like to live with lots of trees nearby. They shelter our houses, yards, and streets. They give a forest feeling to parks and riverbanks and lakes. Trees beautify busy roads and soften their noise.

Many trees in town grow wild, as they did before we occupied the land. These native species plant themselves with help from wind and birds and animals.

Many a favorite yard tree is part of this wild town forest. A seed lands in some odd corner, safe from the mower. It sprouts and grows unnoticed for a year or so. Quietly, but quickly too, it reaches for the light. Then one day someone sees it and says: "What a fine little tree! We must take care of it!"

Town forests are also rich in trees we plant where we want them. These "tame" trees can be native or imported kinds. Either

way, we give them special care, since we've done what nature doesn't do: dig trees up and ask them not to mind.

Of course a tree must grow where it is. It can't pick up and leave! It must adapt or die. A tree that lives a tree's long life must survive a lot of change. Trees that live with people have some strange adventures, as you'll see.

This book describes just seven of the many kinds of trees found all across North America. Ailanthuses and ginkgos are from Asia. Our native maples, willows, syca-

10

mores, oaks, and pines appear as various species, depending on where you live.

Read this book, then take a walk. Count trees and kinds of trees. (Later you can learn their names.) You'll find a mix of wild and tame. You'll see how often the oldest trees are the loveliest. Choose some favorites. Plan to study them all year round. You'll learn their ways and uncover mysteries. You'll find yourself knowing the stories trees tell—of greening and growing for the longest time.

Living~Fossil Ginkgo

THE GINKGO TREE is tough. Two hundred million years ago it lived with dinosaurs. Now it lives with us and our cars. The ginkgo will grow on city streets whose traffic fumes would poison many trees.

The ginkgo leaf looks as ancient as it is. Other tree leaves have branching veins. Ginkgo veins fan out from the stem. The leaf itself looks like a fan, or a duck foot, or a fish fin. It feels like soft leather. It grows on an odd little peg, like an early experiment in attaching leaves to trees.

Fossils show us ginkgos growing for ages all around the world. The age of dinosaurs came and went, but ginkgos stayed. Then, as earth kept changing, new kinds of trees replaced the old. The ginkgo almost joined the forest of extinct trees we now know only as fossil species.

Luckily, several thousand years ago, the Chinese saw a beauty in the odd old ginkgo tree. It was rarely found in the wild, so they grew it in temple gardens. That saved the ginkgo. And now that our cities need tough trees, ginkgos grow all

around the world again.

Female ginkgo trees bear nuts whose fleshy husks smell awful when they fall. Cities avoid that problem by planting the male trees only. Ginkgos in autumn turn a lovely soft yellow. Once you start picking up leaves to keep, it's hard to stop! You think of that ancient ginkgo forest. Dinosaurs must have shuffled through drifts of these same yellow leaves. Now people run over them, parking their cars. . . .

Maple With and Without Leaves

MAPLES are loved for their leafy ways. Those with open spreading limbs cast dappled dancing shadows. Those with full thick crowns form pools of dark, still shade. Some maple leaves show flickering silvery undersides. Some glow red or purple all summer long. People drive miles to see maples turning gorgeous autumn colors.

When maples shed, we see all the nests their leaves helped hide. A robin's mud bowl still hugs its limb. Woodpeckers pecked five holes! The bag the orioles wove swings from its slender twigs. Way up high, two tiny nests tease our curiosity. Maybe a storm will give us one.

Hollows form where big old maples have lost a limb. Owls, raccoons, or possums may move in. Handsome shelf fungi fill hollows too. They feed for years on dead heartwood, hollowing more of the tree. The fungi spread by shedding spores. Fine as dust, they ride the wind— millions of them, so a few can land on the right dead wood.

Maples spread by flying too. Their seeds hang in pairs, like tadpoles nose to nose. They break apart to fly away, whirling in the wind. Hundreds sprout hopeful little maples. Thousands drift in gutters and litter lawns, feeding birds and squirrels. Mice hide tiny piles of them in old bird nests and under logs. Look to see how mice save space—how they nibble away the papery wings of the maple seeds they store.

Mighty Oak
From Little Acorn

FIND ACORNS and you've found an oak. All acorns have the nut in the cup that holds it to the twig. But each kind of oak has its acorn design. Some cups are frilly, some are plain. Nuts may ripen black or brown or tan. Some cups almost hide the nut. Some nuts jut boldly out.

Species in the red-oak group take two years to ripen bitter acorns. Red oaks have sharply pointed leaves. White-oak species have more rounded leaves. Their sweeter-tasting acorns ripen in a year.

Acorns fall at summer's end. Birds and animals scramble to get their share of nuts so easily cracked, so packed with meat.

And the acorn feast can be made to last. Jays hide their winter supply in old nests and hollow trees. Chipmunks store theirs underground. Squirrels bury acorns one by one, *dib-dab, pat-pat*. Many oaks grow from acorns lost or forgotten!

Fallen acorns may be heavy with meat or light with rot. Exit hole and empty shell mean weevil's child has eaten well.

Study the oak that gives you acorns.

Could it grow in some place you know? Would there be sun and soil and room for a sturdy oak to build for a hundred years or more? Would its spreading crown of shining leaves cast a welcome shade?

Say you plant acorns and they sprout. Pull one seedling gently, gently up. See how the nut feeds root and shoot. Think how wonderful it is: that old and mighty oaks have these little acorn beginnings.

Ailanthus
in Odd Hard Places

AILANTHUS succeeds where life for a tree is very hard. It begins with papery seeds spinning along in the winds that sweep down city canyons. Most of the ground there is paved. Rock-hard buildings crowd up into the sky. Yet trees need land and light!

Most ailanthus seeds are lost—crushed underfoot, swept up with trash, washed away. Birds and mice eat some. But some get lucky. They stick in hospitable cracks in the city's hard surface. They land in vacant lots, in spots too rough or steep to mow. They spin down into tiny yards, snug up against a wall.

25

Ailanthuses grow quickly, throwing out long leaves, each a stem with rows of leaflets. When such leaves fall, such graceful plumes, the tree seems much too bare. It appears to poke at the sky with awkward sticks. Bold scars show where the leaves let go. Shy buds rest nearby, where new and larger plumes will rise.

Ailanthuses bloom in spring, females and males on separate trees. The male blooms stink! The females bear heavy tas-

sels of green seed propellers blushed with pink. The seeds hang on, brown and dry, ready to fly through winter into spring. Set some flying on a windy day. Compare the twisting flight of ailanthus with the silken parachute soaring of dandelion or milkweed seeds. See how differently they land. Then find the oddest, hardest growing space any ailanthus tree has claimed in your neighborhood.

Willow Can Come Home With You

Willows love water wherever they live. When they grow on the bank of a river, stream, or pond, you can see their tufty pink roots reaching in to drink. There's nothing like a big old leaning willow for sitting under next to water. Next best is any weeping willow anywhere. It rises like a fountain, spilling a soft green waterfall of long yellow twigs. Viceroy butterflies visit willows to lay their eggs. You can guess why the viceroy caterpillar looks like a bird dropping left on a leaf!

Everyone loves pussy-willow twigs. Even in a vase, the soft furry buds open into dangling blooms called catkins. All

willows have catkins that ripen and launch huge numbers of tiny fluffy seeds. They float on the air and travel far. Lucky ones land where the ground stays moist.

More than a hundred species of willow are native to North America. Many more have been introduced. If you see a willow you like—take it home with you. Ask the owner to give you a start. A few twigs from the tree will do. (Fallen twigs may

not be alive.) Root your start in water in good light. Then plant it away from the plumbing. Thirsty willow roots have a way of sneaking into pipes and drains.

If you race with a growing willow, you'll have to climb to catch up! Willows grow faster than most trees. One cut down may sprout again and again from the roots. Some willows you know may have lived this way for centuries.

Storybark of Sycamore

YOU CAN TELL a sycamore from far away, even from a moving car. The upper limbs show through the leaves with a ghostly gleam of smooth white bark. Sycamores in sooty city air gleam gray, like ghosts that need a wash. Close up, we see the handsome patchwork look of sycamores. It comes from smooth new bark appearing as old bark loosens and falls in strips and shapes like potato chips.

Sycamore leaves can grow quite large. Some are a handful, as you'll find when they come sailing down in the fall. Notice their powdery feel, their unmistakable perfume. You can close your eyes and sniff the air and tell if sycamores are near. Study a number of leaves from any one tree. See how they vary in size and detail. Yet all are alike. All have the sycamore pattern of branching veins that carry sap and give the leaf its strength.

The American sycamore and its cousin, the European plane tree, are planted in cities everywhere. They tolerate polluted air. Given room, they grow lofty crowns of spacious limbs. They also survive being cut to fit a cramped and risky street life. Car bumpers bump them. Tall trucks break limbs. Crews lop and chop to clear utility wires. Roadwork tears into roots growing in so little soil.

Many a story of sycamore life is written, easy to read, in its smooth bark. A bird flies into a hole in a donut-shaped swelling of new bark. We see how a limb once stuck out there, then died or was cut

off short. Then it rotted away, leaving a
hole. Bark hurried to close it, but rot won
the race—lucky for a nesting bird.

That same old sycamore has a hollow
trunk split open partway up. We sniff the
good leaf-mold smell inside, and the mys-
terious rich aroma all sycamores have.
The ancient tree leans and has lost big
limbs to age and storms. Yet it will live
and gleam for years to come.

Pine for Evergreen

EVERYONE knows the sharp sweet smell of pines. It comes from resin, the sap we see oozing from their wounds. Resin is wickedly sticky, so handle with care. Wear old clothes for hugging pines!

Pine leaves are so thin we call them needles. Pines do grow in warm climates, but their waxy slim needles really beat the cold. They dodge bitter winds and don't dry out as tender broad leaves would. This is why winter pines are green while most broad leaf trees stand bare.

Pines are conifers, or cone-bearing trees. Spring winds blow fine yellow pollen from pine to pine. Pollen helps form seed in developing cones. Each kind of pine has its size and shape of cone. Most fit in a squirrel's paws, but when the big cones fall—don't get hit!

Green cone scales fit tight as they grow, each clasping two seeds. The cone ripens brown, then lifts its scales to let seeds go. Most pine seeds are winged and wind sown. Squirrels help by gathering cones to hoard. See how it goes. Throw cones

high on a windy day. Thanks to you a seed may fly and find someplace to pine.

Evergreen pines let old needles fall as new ones come on. The old brown needles spread a fragrant pine straw bed. There's no better place to lie, looking up through branches and out at sky. A pine is so peaceful when the air is still. And pine needles sift the wind with sounds that have no name.

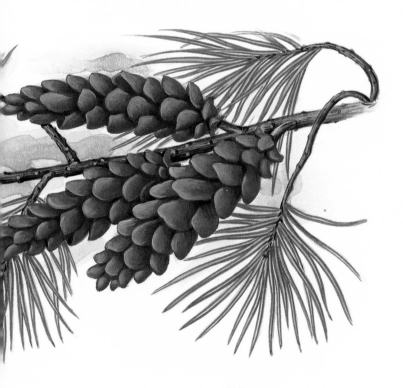

The Living Tree We Never See

How CAN TREES be heavy as whales and still hold themselves sky-high? What must their roots be like? To see all the roots of a fair-sized tree, you'd have to wash away tons of soil. There could be rocks and other entangling roots. And the tree would die. It couldn't show how roots go on adventuring underground for all of a long, long life. We wouldn't see how roots, like leaves, twigs, and limbs, are growing and changing all the time.

Yet science has uncovered fascinating clues to the mystery of roots. We know, for example, that roots meet and merge to share resources. They share with fungi

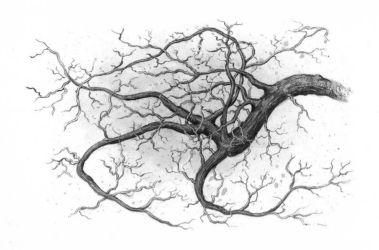

and bacteria, too. Some roots use chemicals to defend their growing space.

We used to picture roots digging down deep to hold a tree upright. Some trees do have a deep, carrotlike taproot. But now we know that most of a tree's root growth occurs in the top eighteen inches of soil. Roots of a healthy tree roam far beyond the spread of branches overhead. Think how hard it is for roots to forage under concrete. Think how they suffer when we dig needless holes, or drive over grass to park in the shade.

Roots do far more than hold a tree upright. They send water and minerals up to the leaves and store food sent down to them. The tree we see is healthy thanks to the one we must imagine—a tree of busily branching roots, searching the earth unseen.

Every Leaf
Works for Life

Earth is a green-plant planet. On land, and floating in the sea, green plants keep the whole world eating. Only they can use the light of our star, the sun, to create new food energy. One way or another, every living thing on earth depends on plants for food.

Green plants also give earth its life-sustaining oxygen. As they make their own food, plants release this vital gas. Most living things breathe in oxygen and breathe out carbon dioxide. Plants recycle that carbon-dioxide "waste," using it and water to make more food. In doing that, plants release more oxygen. . . .

All this wonderful green-plant work is done with energy from the sun, so it's called photosynthesis. That means using-light-to-put-things-together. The green pigment chlorophyll is in charge—the green of our green-plant planet.

No wonder giant plants like trees hold out so many leaves. Each leaf is a sunlight catcher, sugar baker, oxygen maker. But

working leaves do wear out. Trees we call deciduous shed them in the fall. Trees we call evergreen grow new leaves before they shed the old.

Study the leaves on your favorite tree. Take along a picnic lunch. Look up and breathe in deep. Think how green is the color of life and breath on earth—the color of lunch.

The Tree Outside and in Your Guide

Every lover of trees needs a guidebook to help identify them. A guide for beginners will cover more than a hundred common trees. More advanced guides cover all eight hundred species native to North America. Study the many guides bookstores and libraries have. Then buy your favorite—the guide you'll use for years outside.

Nurseries, gardeners, and gardening books help us identify non-native trees. Gardens of trees, called arboretums, grow trees from around the world, as do botanical gardens. Both offer tree walks and talks. So do many museums, state and national parks, and nature centers.